DEADLY DISASTERS

Earthquakes

Disaster & Survival

Jennifer Reed

 Enslow Publishers, Inc.

40 Industrial Road   PO Box 38
Box 398   Aldershot
Berkeley Heights, NJ 07922   Hants GU12 6BP
USA   UK

http://www.enslow.com

Library of Congress Cataloging-in-Publication Data:

Reed, Jennifer.
    Earthquakes : disaster & survival / Jennifer Bond Reed.
       p. cm. — (Deadly disasters)
    Includes bibliographical references and index.
    ISBN 0-7660-2381-8
    1. Earthquakes—Juvenile literature. I. Title. II. Series.
QE521.3.R44   2004
363.34'95—dc22

                         2004011698

Printed in the United States of America

10 9 8 7 6 5 4 3 2

To Our Readers: We have done our best to make sure all Internet addresses in this book were active and appropriate when we went to press. However, the author and the publisher have no control over and assume no liability for the material available on those Internet sites or on other Web sites they may link to. Any comments or suggestions can be sent by e-mail to comments@enslow.com or to the address on the back cover.

Illustration Credits: Associated Press, Anatolia, p. 4; Associated Press, AP, pp. 7, 15, 23, 32, 36, 37, 39; Enslow Publishers, Inc., p. 13; European PressPhoto Agency, EPA, pp. 27, 40; Gary Hincks/Science Photo Library, p. 11; Karl V. Steinbrugge Collection, Earthquake Engineering Research Center, p. 20; Library of Congress, Prints and Photographs Division, p. 33; NASA Photo, p. 14; NOAA/Department of Commerce, p. 31; NOAA/EDIS, p. 18; Associated Press, AP, p. 1; Painet Photos, p. 25; U.S. Geological Survey, pp. 9, 24.

Cover Illustration: Associated Press, AP.

Contents

1 Living Dangerously 5

2 What Is an Earthquake? 10

3 Central and
South America 17

4 Asia and the Middle East 22

5 North America 29

6 Saving Lives 34

Top Ten Deadliest Earthquakes Ever 42

Chapter Notes 43

Glossary 46

Further Reading
and Internet Addresses 47

Index 48

A fire-fighting plane is dwarfed by thick clouds of smoke coming from the Tupras oil refinery in Izmit, Turkey. The fire was caused by the 1999 earthquake.

Living Dangerously

A HOWLING DOG WOKE PINAR ONUK SUDDENLY around 3:00 A.M. Another loud noise pierced the night. The next thing Pinar knew, her home was leaning toward the house next door: ". . . I could even see right into the other house from the window . . . There was an incredible groaning noise. That noise was my friend in the house opposite, who was trapped under a cupboard."[1]

A Vacation Gone Wrong

Pinar was visiting her grandmother in Sapanca, Turkey. It was summer vacation. Sapanca is located in the northwest part of the country.

Pinar Onuk did not know what was happening. At first, the shaking seemed to stop, but it had not. She later said, "It was as if something had grabbed hold of us from underneath, turned us upside down and was shaking us."[2] Noises came from the ground. Pinar wanted to find her mother but she could not move. In fact, she could not feel her feet. Cries and breaking glass echoed in the darkness. To Pinar it seemed as if the movement would never cease. However, the earthquake quickly ended. Pinar heard her mother call for her. Her feet "revived" and she ran to her mother's arms. Unfortunately, the nightmare had only begun for her family as well as tens of thousands of people living in Turkey.

Ertunga Gamiz, a young boy, also heard dogs outside. "I woke up in the night with the screaming and the sounds of dogs barking. There was a terrible shaking. I was very frightened."[3] Ertunga clearly remembered how there was no electricity and people walked around with candles.

On August 17, 1999, at 3:02 A.M., one of Turkey's largest earthquakes struck with complete devastation. In fact, the 7.4 magnitude earthquake, which was centered near the quiet port of Izmit, was one of the largest of the twentieth century. Oil refineries burst into flames during the forty-five-second earthquake. Around Izmit, villages and towns were wiped out.

The Devastation

Chaos broke out all over northwestern Turkey. People scrambled to save loved ones under the rubble. Silence crept over the towns and villages as people hushed their voices. They listened for calls for help. Then sirens, dogs, screams, and cries were heard. Some cries were of joy as children, husbands, and wives were pulled to safety. Others were cries of sorrow as body after body was pulled from the wreckage. It is estimated that over sixteen thousand people died and over twenty thousand were injured.

Thousands of buildings were turned into rubble. Explosions erupted and fires burned. Disease spread

With the help of a bulldozer, rescue workers in Izmit, Turkey try to dig through concrete rubble to find survivors.

because of the corpses. There was still no electricity or clean water. People roamed the streets not knowing where to go or what to do. Children were orphaned; people lost their homes. Yet despite the terrible conditions, neighbors helped neighbors and people pulled together. They celebrated when people were found alive. They helped strangers recover their belongings and mourned the loss of their own loved ones.

Ismail Cimen was one of the last survivors found alive. Just four years old, he was trapped for six days in the remains of his home in Cinarcik. He had only an inch of space above his face. Journalists and photographers flocked to his bedside in the hospital. He was the face of hope.[4]

Earthquakes in Turkey

Earthquakes are a common occurrence in northern Turkey. There, the North Anatolian Fault runs from west to east. A fault is a crack in the earth's crust where rock has shifted. When the earthquake of August 1999 hit, it was not the largest earthquake recorded in this area. In 1939, an earthquake measuring 8.0 occurred along the fault. However, it caused much less damage and loss of life because it occurred in a more remote area.

The loss of life and damage in the earthquake of 1999 was high because it occurred in a very populated area. Also, many buildings were unable to handle the tremors

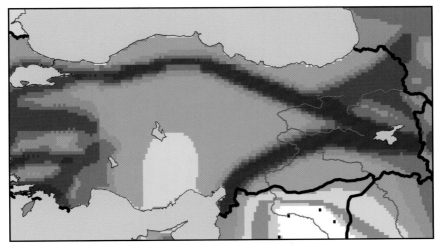

This map of Turkey shows earthquake activity. The red and brown areas have the most earthquakes. The curved red and brown line at the top traces the North Anatolian Fault.

beneath them. Some older buildings, such as the Blue Mosque and Topkaki Palace, survived. They had little damage because they were stronger. Meanwhile, brand-new buildings collapsed. Building engineers and city planners were blamed for poor construction.

Earthquakes Throughout the World

Better building materials and designs could have helped prevent this devastation in Turkey. There is no way to predict exactly when and where an earthquake will strike. Scientists study earthquakes around the world so that they can teach people how to prepare for them. It is important for people to know how earthquakes work in order to understand why they cause such great devastation.

CHAPTER 2

What Is an Earthquake?

EVERY THIRTY SECONDS THERE IS A TREMOR somewhere on the earth, totaling over five hundred thousand tremors a year. Roughly, one hundred thousand of these can be felt by humans and about one hundred cause damage.[1]

Fortunately, the majority of these quakes occur in the ocean crust or in areas where few people live. When an earthquake does hit a major city or populated area, the damage may be great.

How Does an Earthquake Happen?

Earthquakes occur because of the movement of the earth's tectonic plates. The earth's crust and upper mantle are made of several large, rigid plates that move relative to one another. Plates are in constant motion. They are found under the oceans (oceanic plates) or under the continents (continental plates). Because these plates are moving, they cause stress in the earth's crust. A crack appears where rock has shifted. This crack is called a fault line. The focus or point of origin of an earthquake is located beneath the surface.

About 90 percent of all earthquakes are produced at plate boundaries where two plates are colliding, spreading apart, or sliding past each other.[2] Earthquake waves resemble sound and water waves in the way in which they move. If a rock is dropped into a puddle, the ripples

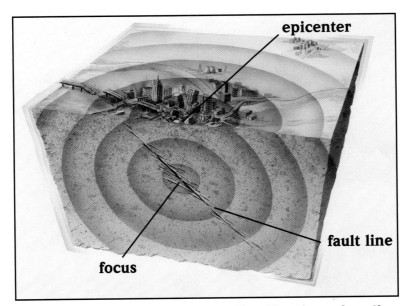

Earthquakes happen along a fault line. The place where the earthquake originates is the focus. The point directly above the focus on the surface is the epicenter.

in the water resemble the earthquake waves that roll through the earth's crust. This rippling effect often damages anything on the surface.

The movement sends shock waves through surrounding rock in many directions. These seismic waves are energy that can penetrate rock. They cause the earth to shake and heave. The force of these waves depends on how deep the focus is and the strength of the surrounding rock. The epicenter is located on the surface of the earth and is directly above the focus. The greatest amount of damage does not always occur at the epicenter. Sometimes it happens miles away.

Seismology

The study of earthquakes is called seismology. Scientists called seismologists use many instruments to determine where an earthquake is centered and how strong it is. Some of these instruments include satellites, seismometers, seismographs, borehole tiltmeters, and seismic trucks.

People have been studying earthquakes for thousands of years. In A.D. 130, a Chinese astronomer named Zhang Heng invented the first instrument for detecting earthquakes. This was the first seismometer. It had eight dragons on top and eight bronze frogs at the base. Each dragon held a ball. When the earth shook, one of the balls

The first seismometer was created in A.D. 130. It was decorated with images of dragons and frogs.

dropped and landed in the mouth of one of the frogs below.[3]

Later, in 1760, the British engineer, John Michell, wrote that earthquakes and the waves of energy that they make are caused by "shifting masses of rock miles below the surface."[4] Even though he did not have the technology or instruments used today, he was right.

Earthquakes are measured by their intensity and magnitude. Intensity measures the effect on the earth: shaking of the ground, buildings, and natural features. Magnitude measures the energy released. The Richter scale is sometimes used to measure and compare the magnitude of earthquakes. It is a measure of the strength of the seismic waves sent out from the focus of the earthquake.[5] There are many other scales used today to determine the magnitude and intensity of an earthquake. A moment magnitude scale, or M, was also developed. For very large earthquakes, moment magnitude gives the most reliable estimate of

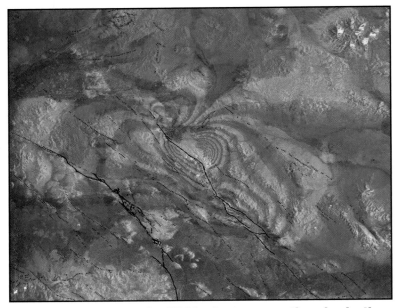

This satellite image by NASA shows an earthquake in the Hector Mine in California that occurred on October 16, 1999. The earthquake was 7.1 magnitude. However, it occurred in an unpopulated area and did not cause much damage.

earthquake size. An instrument called a seismograph measures and records the strength of an earthquake. The higher the number of magnitude, the stronger the earthquake.

Satellites help scientists detect movements of the earth's tectonic plates. Each satellite bounces laser beams between the earth and itself.

Where Do Most Earthquakes Occur?

There are two major regions of earthquake activity on the earth. One is the Pacific belt. It encircles the Pacific

14

Ocean. The other is the Alpine belt, which slices through Europe and Asia. The Pacific belt includes the west coasts of North America and South America, Japan, and the Philippines. "The western edge of the Pacific Ocean and the west coast of South America are the place where the relative motion between plates is greatest. So there are more and larger earthquakes there," says Jeff Barker, associate professor of geophysics at SUNY, Binghamton, New York. "China has large earthquakes, mostly as a

This seismologist in Taiwan is studying readings from a recent earthquake.

result of the collision of India with Asia, which resulted in the uplift of the Himalaya Mountains."[6]

Determining Where an Earthquake May Occur

Earthquakes occur at three kinds of plate boundary: ocean ridges where the plates are pulled apart, margins where the plates scrape past one another, and margins where one plate is thrust into the other. Scientists can predict the general regions on the earth's surface where they can expect large earthquakes in the future. These regions cover 10 percent of the earth's surface.

Often there are smaller earthquakes called foreshocks and aftershocks. Foreshocks occur before a major quake, while aftershocks occur after. The bigger the earthquake, the bigger and stronger the aftershocks. However, these aftershocks are less strong than the actual earthquake.

Along with the study of earthquakes, it is also important to hear the stories of those who have survived earthquakes.

CHAPTER 3

Central and South America

EARTHQUAKES ARE COMMON ON THE WEST COAST of South America and parts of Central America, including Mexico and Guatemala. There is a great oceanic plate under the Pacific Ocean. It is colliding with the South American plate.

In recent years, Central and South America have been home to three large earthquakes. On June 9, 1994, in northern Bolivia, the earth shook so violently that houses and buildings crumbled. Landslides destroyed villages. The earthquake had a magnitude of 8.2. It was the first earthquake from this part of South America to be felt in North America. There were only five people killed, but there were numerous reports of damage.[1]

An Earthquake's Deadly Product

On July 30, 1995, in Chile, another huge earthquake struck, killing three people and destroying entire towns. It had a magnitude of 8.2.[2] This violent earthquake created a tsunami, which was seen as far away as Hawaii and California.

Tsunamis form when an offshore earthquake moves the ocean bottom in a vertical direction—up or down. Waves of water then move toward the coast, growing larger as the water near shore becomes shallower. They can move as quickly as 800 kilometers per hour (500 miles per hour). Once they hit land, they can be many feet high. One of the largest and most devastating tsunamis hit

The man on the left is about to be hit by a tsunami, which is breaking over a pier in Hilo Harbor, Hawaii. The man did not survive the April 1, 1946 tsunami.

Alaska in 1958. The waves at Lituya Bay measured over 525 meters (over 1,700 feet) high and killed 115 people.[3]

Landslides in El Salvador

The twenty-first century has already seen its share of devastation. When a 7.6 magnitude earthquake hit El Salvador in January 2001, many of the poorly built homes there collapsed, killing and trapping hundreds of people. The earthquake also triggered landslides, which demolished buildings and buried villages. "This is terrible. I don't think we will be able to pull out any victims; everything has been buried," said David Lara, a rescue worker.[4]

"I felt an earthquake and all the hill came down and covered the houses," said Candido Salinas, a sixty-year-old man who lived across the street from the slide zone. A slide zone is the area where the land slides down the hill.[5]

Peru

On Saturday, June 23, 2001, an earthquake hit Peru. It measured between 7.9 and 8.1 magnitude. It was a quiet afternoon. Many people were relaxing at home because it was a weekend. Suddenly, the earth "rolled liked waves," said one survivor.[6] People fled from their homes as

> **"Please help us, we've lost everything."**
>
> —Maria Luis Arbuli, earthquake survivor.

19

A 1970 earthquake caused an avalanche in Yungay, Peru. Both of the photos were taken from the same spot—before (top) and after (bottom) the earthquake.

fast as they could. "Please help us, we've lost everything," wailed Maria Luis Arbului, whose house was destroyed. "The rocks took my bed and my furniture and now I'm left out on the street."[7] Like Maria, hundreds of thousands of people were left homeless.

Earthquakes can have a ripple affect. Often they trigger other life-threatening events. In 1970, a magnitude 7.9 earthquake in the Peruvian Andes caused a large mass of ice and rock to separate from a vertical face on Nevado Huascaran, the highest peak in Peru. The slab fell 1,000 meters (3,281 feet). At this point a mixture of crushed rock and melted ice, the debris reached a speed as high as 280 kilometers (174 miles) per hour. It split around a small hill and buried the towns of Yungay and Ranrahirca. The death toll in both villages was twenty thousand.

However, there are other places in the world with devastating earthquakes. Asia and the Middle East have also had to deal with these damaging natural disasters.

CHAPTER

4

Asia and the Middle East

IN LESS THAN A MINUTE, THOUSANDS OF BUILDINGS were reduced to rubble. Thriving communities were demolished and people scrambled for their lives. Another major earthquake had rocked the country of Taiwan.

Taiwan, an island located off the coast of China, was shaken awake on Tuesday morning, September 21, 1999. The magnitude was 7.6 and the quake hit at 1:47 A.M. A death toll of seventeen hundred was recorded. Close to four thousand people were injured. Many earthquakes strike Taiwan each year. However, an earthquake of this size was a surprise. The last one to occur with this force was in 1986 with a magnitude of 7.8.

The Ring of Fire

Asia is part of the Pacific Rim, or Ring of Fire. The Pacific Rim includes the western coast of the United States, as well as Alaska and Hawaii. The Ring of Fire is known for its strong earthquakes and volcanic action. Countries like Japan, Korea, China, Indonesia, and Australia all feel the effects from time to time.

This hotel collapsed in Taipei, Taiwan, during the 1999 earthquake. Workers try to hose down fires within the building.

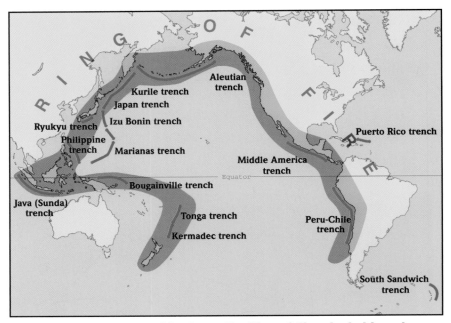

This computer graphic shows the Ring of Fire shaded in red. Green lines represent oceanic trenches. These trenches are formed when one tectonic plate slides under another.

Chaos in Kobe

On January 17, 1995, in Kobe, Japan, nearly sixty-three hundred people died. The world was surprised because Japan, a nation known for its earthquakes, was generally well prepared for such an event. On this fateful day, several things happened that took even the most well-prepared people by surprise.

Kobe is a large port city, and the biggest city located between the dangerous intersection of three tectonic plates: the Pacific, Eurasian, and Philippine. It lies in a highly earthquake-prone area. The magnitude of the 1995 earthquake was 7.2.

Because Kobe is located near the coast, the soil is soft and contains a lot of water. The earthquake destroyed the water supply, train lines, and roads that entered the city. Many buildings collapsed. Fires broke out all over the city.[1] Without a water supply to put out the fires, many people died. Thousands were left homeless in the middle of winter. Many elderly people died from the cold. Children went hungry.

Rescue and Recovery

In Nishinomiya, Lieutenant Tsutomu Fujii and ten of his men from the Japanese Self-Defense Forces toiled through a frigid night. They dug out the bodies of a little girl's parents as she sat crying nearby. Lieutenant Fujii had uncovered seven corpses since morning. "That couple seems to have got out of bed and made it to the entryway of their house," he said. "Then the whole house fell on them. They didn't stand a chance."[2]

High Casualties in Iran

A more recent earthquake occurred on December 26, 2003, in Bam, Iran. The earthquake had a magnitude of 6.7. At least twenty-six thousand bodies were recovered.

Tens of thousands more were injured. Entire villages of mud-brick houses collapsed.

Mostafa Biderani and his wife, Zahra Nazari, wept in front of a destroyed police station in the center of Bam. Biderani had driven from Isfahan, 470 miles to the northwest. "But all my hopes were dashed when I saw the police station had collapsed," he said, "I pulled out my son with my bare hands."[3]

Walls of Water

The fourth largest earthquake in the world since 1900 caused devastating damage on December 26, 2004.[4] Located off the coast of northern Sumatra, Indonesia, in the Indian Ocean, the 9.0 magnitude earthquake created powerful tsunamis.

The Indonesian island is familiar with earthquakes. They happen frequently. To understand the power of this earthquake, some scientists have compared it to the power of a million atomic bombs.[5] The earthquake did damage buildings on the Indonesian island, but the real devastation was more widespread and occurred from the tsunamis the earthquake created.

Tsunamis are very rare in the Indian Ocean. The December 26, 2004, tsunami in the Indian Ocean was the first in that region since 1883, when the Krakatoa volcano exploded.[6] Because they are rare, there was no warning

These photos were taken from video footage of a December 26, 2004 tsunami hitting a resort on Patong Beach in Phuket, Thailand. Notice that the building in the center of the photo is completely destroyed.

system in place. Walls of water plowed on shore in several countries. Indonesia, Thailand, India, and Sri Lanka were hit the hardest.

Peter Heydemann, from Chicago, was vacationing in Thailand when the first wave of tsunamis hit. They flooded the streets. He ventured outside, not knowing that a bigger wave was yet to come. A few minutes later, another tsunami hit. Heydemann was dragged out to sea. All kinds of wreckage floated around him, including wood, pieces of buildings, and gas cans. He was able to grab hold of a body board and floated in the ocean for forty minutes. "It seemed like it was over," he said. "Nobody saw me from the beach. I tried every now and then to let go of the flotation and wave, but nobody could see me."[7] Finally, Heydemann was rescued.

In the middle of January 2005, the total death toll from the Indian Ocean tsunamis was estimated to be over one hundred sixty thousand. It is expected to rise. Five million people were homeless and starving. Although rescue efforts and aid helped, the effect of this earthquake and its tsunamis will be felt for many years.

North America

WHEN A SHIP PULLED INTO THE SMALL HARBOR at Valdez, Alaska, it was a welcome sight. Valdez, located on Prince William Sound, was a small town on the Alaskan shoreline. It was just east of Anchorage. On March 27, 1964, a steamship named *Chena* docked, bringing fresh fruit and vegetables. Many people in town came out to greet *Chena* and her crew. Children stood on the docks to watch the steamship. Crew members tossed oranges to the children.[1] It was a good day—until the earth buckled beneath them.

The Good Friday Quake

The crew had not left the boat when the ground shook. They watched helplessly from the deck as the town's two piers, where children were eating oranges, were sucked into the water. Along with them went buildings, cars, and people who were near the harbor. Waves overtook them and nearly sunk the *Chena*. From on board the ship, "I saw people running—it was just ghastly," M. D. Stewart, captain of the *Chena*, wrote later about the disaster. There was no sign of them."[2] The earthquake that struck did more than shake the ground. It started landslides and tsunamis. The water rose 69.8 meters (229 feet) and swamped the small town. In all, 131 people died—115 in Alaska, and 16 in Oregon and California. Valdez was later rebuilt four miles away at its current site.

> "They were just engulfed by buildings, water, mud and everything . . . that is what has kept me awake for days."
>
> —M.D. Stewart, captain of the *Chena*.

The Good Friday Quake, as some called it, was the strongest earthquake to ever hit North America. It registered 9.2 magnitude. It was the second largest quake ever measured in the world, after the earthquake in Chile in 1960. The damage was huge and cost hundreds of millions of dollars. However, the death toll was low for an earthquake of this size. Alaska had a low population. It was a holiday and many people were home.

Tremors Felt Far and Wide

The epicenter of the quake was about 56 miles west of Valdez and 75 miles east of Anchorage. Tremors were felt

The Good Friday earthquake caused great devastation in Valdez, Alaska. On the left, a boat can be seen washed up on shore after the 1964 quake.

as far as Washington State. Anchorage also suffered severe damage. One survivor wrote about the experience as she sat in a movie theater in downtown Anchorage. She was watching Disney's *The Sword and the Stone*, and as the prince pulled the sword from the stone, the earthquake interrupted the movie. According to the survivor:

> The roaring of the earth was deafening, coming in waves. As the lights were flashing out you could see the seats rolling in peaks of at least four-foot high waves. Then the emergency lights came on. The picture on the screen

31

jumped uncontrollably hitting the ceiling then the floor until the film broke.

It is amazing that many people survived. When they left the theater, the rooftops were at ground level. Schools, shops, homes, and most buildings were destroyed.[3]

California vs. Alaska

The San Andreas Fault runs through California, causing many minor earthquakes. Once in awhile, a large earthquake hits California. In 1906 and 1989, strong earthquakes rocked San Francisco. The 1906 quake and resulting fire

In 1994, an earthquake in California caused part of state Route 14 to collapse. Several vehicles were stranded on part of the highway.

The 1906 earthquake in San Francisco caused a huge fire that lasted for days. A hundred years ago, people were not as prepared for earthquakes as they are today.

destroyed twenty-eight thousand buildings and killed at least three thousand people. Only twelve people died in the 1989 quake.

Many people think that California has the most earthquakes in North America. However, Alaska is the leader. It has had more earthquakes than any other region in the lower forty-nine states combined. Alaska lies on a seismically active boundary. It is exposed to earthquake and volcanic activity.[4]

Whether in California, Alaska, or anywhere else in the world, it is important for people in earthquake-prone areas to be prepared for the worst.

CHAPTER

6

Saving Lives

ALTHOUGH MUCH IS KNOWN ABOUT EARTHQUAKES, technology today is still unable to determine the exact day and location that an earthquake will strike. Forecasts of the approximate locations and magnitudes of some future large earthquakes can be made. Most large earthquakes occur on long fault zones around the margin of the western Pacific Ocean. This is because the Atlantic Ocean is growing a few inches wider each year, and the Pacific is shrinking as ocean floor is pushed beneath the Pacific Rim continents.[1]

Earthquake Predictions?

The best way today to predict an earthquake is to study areas that have a history of quakes. Some signs that could be useful in predicting an earthquake include: foreshocks, changes in groundwater chemistry; pressure of fluids in underground rocks; creep, the slow movement along faults; earthquakes that occur in other parts of a fault; changes in local magnetic field; and strain in underground rocks. Areas that show increased activity also may have a bigger earthquake. If there is unusual activity in a particular area, people may be forewarned through the television, radio, and sirens. Experts are also focusing on the structure and materials used in buildings.

Engineers try to create perfect, earthquake-proof homes. Scientists work on producing materials that will hold up to an earthquake's ravage.

Can Animals Predict an Earthquake?

Many people have noticed unusual behavior by domesticated animals before an earthquake. Some examples are the howling dogs in Turkey and ferrets hiding all their toys.

Chinese seismologists collected over two thousand reports of animals acting strangely. They noted that just prior to an earthquake, the unusual activity increased. They also noticed that the bigger the quake, the more strange the behavior. Scientists now believe that animals are more sensitive to foreshocks than humans. They may be able to feel the ground vibrating.[2]

Survival

Being prepared is perhaps the best defense against an earthquake. People living in earthquake-prone areas

Dot Halstead, director of the New Madrid Historical Museum in New Madrid, Missouri, stands beside an earthquake kit. Two major earthquakes hit New Madrid in 1811 and 1812.

should keep an "earthquake kit" in the home and car. The kits should provide food and supplies for three days. The survival kit should have such items as water (two quarts to one gallon per person per day), first aid kit, canned food, medication, blankets, battery-operated radio, flashlight, fire extinguisher, toilet paper, hand soap, plastic plates and utensils, and a pot or two. Every family member should know where the shut-off valves for the gas, water, and electricity are as well as emergency phone numbers. An axe, hammer, screwdriver, shovel, broom, and adhesive tape are also recommended.

What to Do

When an earthquake hits, one should stay calm. If a person is inside, the safest place to be is in a doorway or crouched under a sturdy piece of furniture. Stay away from glass and heavy objects that are not attached to a wall. If someone is caught outside, he or she should stay

These Japanese children are taking part in an earthquake drill in Tokyo.

away from electrical and telephone lines, buildings, and trees. Avoid anything that can fall. If in a car, stay in the vehicle and drive away from overpasses and underpasses, bridges, and tunnels.

After an earthquake has hit, check for injuries and provide first aid if possible. Listen to a radio for additional information. Check for spills like sewage and turn off all the gas, water, and electricity lines. Wearing shoes is important because stepping on glass or nails can cause serious injury.

Search and Rescue

One of the hardest jobs is being a search-and-rescue worker. Brave men and women go into ravaged earthquake areas to find people both dead and alive.

Doug Copp, a member of the American Rescue Team International, knows all too well the devastation caused by earthquakes. He was one of the first Americans on the scene in Turkey. A helicopter took his rescue team high above the devastation. They saw buildings toppled over and observed which ones may have people trapped inside.

> "... My guts are ripped out."
>
> —Rescuer Doug Copp on how his job makes him feel.

In describing how searching for survivors makes him feel, Doug Copp says, " . . . my guts are ripped out."[3]

38

Rescue workers look for victims of the 1995 earthquake in Kobe, Japan.

Yet Copp is committed to saving lives. With other rescue workers, Copp heard muffled screams coming from an apartment building. A search began through slabs of concrete and rubble. Using sensitive microphones, Copp and the rescue workers listened. As the night wore on, the screams were no longer heard. The team moved to another area and searched for living victims.

Rubble was removed piece by piece. Not only does the team need to know how to remove rubble so that other pieces do not come crashing down, they must also be skilled in medicine. Broken bones and dehydration plague many victims trapped in an earthquake.

Despite the loss of life, there were happy moments, too. Doug Copp and his team saved a young girl's life. "My heart was soaring right to the top of the sky . . . Sometimes in life there's moments and those moments are special, and there were some special moments then."[4]

This dog is being used by a Norwegian rescue team to search for victims of the 2003 earthquake in Bam, Iran.

Help with Dogs

Search and rescue does not just involve people. In almost every earthquake, dogs are brought in to search for people. Dogs can catch a smell of a person, even if the person is buried or underwater.

Dogs let their handlers know if they have found a person by barking, whining, or scratching. Some are even trained to tell the handler if the person is dead or alive.

Living With Earthquakes

The fact remains that each year thousands of people die in earthquakes. It is not easy to accept. The human factor makes this natural occurrence so tragic. However, the more that people are educated, the more likely they are to survive. As people build better and stronger earthquake-proof homes, there is hope for less loss of life in the future.

Top Ten Deadliest Earthquakes Ever

Rank	Date	Place	Deaths	Magnitude
1.	January 23, 1556	China, Shansi	830,000	about 8
2.	July 27, 1976	China, Tangshan	255,000	7.5
3.	August 9, 1138	Syria, Aleppo	230,000	unknown
4.	May 22, 1927	China, near Xining	200,000	7.9
5.	December 22, 856	Iran, Damghan	200,000	unknown
6.	December 16, 1920	China, Gansu	200,000	8.6
7.	December 26, 2004	Area around the Indian Ocean	at least 160,000*	9.0
8.	March 23, 893	Iran, Ardabil	150,000	unknown
9.	September 1, 1923	Japan, Kwanto	143,000	7.9
10.	October 5, 1948	USSR (Turkmenistan, Ashgabat)	110,000	7.3

Statistics from the U.S. Geological Survey Earthquake Hazards Program <http://neic.usgs.gov/neis/eqlists/eqsmosde.html>

*This is an estimated total. Final casualties for this earthquake may be higher.

Chapter Notes

Chapter 1. Living Dangerously

1. "Children and the Earthquake in Turkey," *The Turkey Research Center*, n.d., <http://www.turkeyresearch.com/earthquake/index.html> (December 11, 2003).

2. Ibid.

3. Ibid.

4. "The Tales of the Earthquake Survivors," *BBC News*, August 23, 1999, <http://news.bbc.co.uk/1/hi/world/europe/428264.stm> (December 11, 2003).

Chapter 2. What Is an Earthquake?

1. Cool Earthquake Facts, U.S. Geological Survey, n.d., <http://earthquakes.usgs.gov/4kids/facts.html> (December 11, 2003).

2. Ibid.

3. Ibid.

4. Ibid.

5. The Severity of an Earthquake, U.S. Geological Survey, n.d., <http://pubs.usgs.gov/gip/earthq4/severitygip.html> (December 11, 2003).

6. Interview with Jeff Barker, Associate Professor of Geophysics, SUNY, Binghamton, March 16, 2003.

Chapter 3. Central and South America

1. "The Largest Earthquakes in the World in the Past 10 Years: 1989 to 1998," U.S. Geological Survey, n.d., <http://wwwneic.cr.usgs.gov/neis/eqlists/last_big10.html> (December 11, 2003).

2. Ibid.

3. 1964 Alaskan Tsunami, USC Tsunami Research Group, n.d., <http://www.usc.edu/dept/tsunamis/index.html> (December 8, 2003).

4. "Major Earthquake rocks Central America," *CNN*, January 13, 2001, <http://europe.cnn.com/2001/world/americas/01/13/quake.03> (December 11, 2003).

5. Ibid.

6. "Race to Find Peru Quake Survivors," *BBC News*, June 24, 2001, <http://news.bbc.co.uk/1/hi/world/americas/1405287.stm> (December 11, 2003).

7. Ibid.

Chapter 4. Asia and the Middle East

1. "Earthquake Effects. Kobe, Japan," by J. Louie, October 9, 1996, <http://www.seismo.unr.edu/ftp/pub/louie/class/100/effects-kobe.html> (December 11, 2003).

2. May Lee, "Kobe Mourns and Struggles," *CNN World News*, January 17, 1996, <http://www.cnn.com/world/9601/kobe/01-17> (December 11, 2003).

3. "40,000 feared dead in Iran," *CBS/AP*, December 29, 2003, <http://www.cbsnews.com/stories/2003/12/26/world/main590242.shtml> (December 29, 2003).

4. USGS Earthquake Hazards Program, December 30, 2004, <http://earthquake.usgs.gov/eqinthenews/2004/usslav/> (December 31, 2004).

5. "Quakes Power = million atomic bombs?," *CNN*, December 29, 2004, <http://www.cnn.com/2004/TECH/science/12/27/quake.seismic.ap/> (December 31, 2004).

6. Ibid.

7. "Survivors Tsunami Horror," *India Daily*, December 30, 2004, <http://www.indiadaily.com/breaking_news/18881.asp> (December 31, 2004).

Chapter 5. North America

1. "Anniversary: The Great Alaska Earthquake of 1964," Tuesday, March 27, 2001, <http://www.disasterrelief.org/Disasters/010326alaskaquake1964/> (December 23, 2003).

2. Ibid.

3. "1964 Alaska Earthquake," personal story, n.d., <http://www.alaska1959.com/1964Earthquake.html> (December 23, 2003).

4. Impact of the 1964 Great Alaskan Earthquake on local areas: Earthquake History of Alaska, Brandon Green, March 1, 2001, <http://www.owlnet.rice.edu/~geol108/eq19/Alaska_Hist/EQHistory> (December 23, 2003).

Chapter 6. Saving Lives

1. Ruth Ludwin, "Earthquake Prediction," The Pacific Northwest Seismograph Network, November 13, 2002, <http://www.geophys.washington.edu/SEIS/PNSN/INFO_GENERAL/eq_prediction.html> (December 11, 2003).

2. T. Neil Davis, "Earthquakes and Animals Article #295," Alaska Science Forum, March 2, 1979, <http://www.gi.alaska.edu/ScienceForum/ASF2/295.html> (December 11, 2003).

3. Prime Time Special, ABC Network, "The World's Deadliest Earthquakes," Doug Copp, American Rescue Team International, <http://www.amerrescue.org.> (December 11, 2003).

4. Ibid.

Glossary

aftershock—Tremors that occur after an earthquake.

borehole tiltmeter—Instrument that records the tilt of the ground.

earthquake—A shaking or trembling of the earth.

epicenter—The point on the surface of the ground above the focus; the center of the earthquake on the ground.

fault line—Cracks in the earth's crust where rocks have shifted.

focus—Point of origin where rocks move. The focus is located beneath the surface of the ground. Also known as hypocenter.

foreshocks—Smaller tremors that occur before a large earthquake.

hypocenter—The location beneath the earth's surface where the rupture of the fault line begins during an earthquake. Also known as focus.

moment magnitude—A number used to measure the size of an earthquake. Moment is a physical quantity proportional to the slip on the fault, times the area of the fault surface that slips; it is related to the total energy released in the earthquake.

plate—Masses of rock below the surface.

Richter scale—A number used to measure the seismic energy of an earthquake.

seismograph—An instrument that measures the amount of ground motion that an earthquake produces.

seismology—The study of earthquakes.

tsunami—A great sea wave caused by earth movement or volcanic eruptions.

Further Reading

Books

Downs, Sandra. *When the Earth Moves*. Brookfield, Conn.: Twenty-First Century Books, 2000.

Morris, Neil. *Earthquakes*. New York: Barrons, 1999.

Prager, Ellen J. *Earthquakes: Jump Into Science*. Washington, D.C.: National Geographic Society, 2002.

Rogers, Daniel. *Earthquakes*. Austin, Tex.: Raintree Steck Vaughn Publishers, 1999.

Sherrow, Victoria. *San Francisco Earthquake: 1989. Death and Destruction*. Springfield, N.J.: Enslow Publishers, Inc., 1998.

Simon, Seymour. *Danger! Earthquakes.* New York: Seastar Books, 2002.

Trveit, Trudi Strain. *Earthquakes*. New York: Franklin Watts, 2003.

Internet Addresses

FEMA for Kids: Earthquakes.
<http://www.fema.gov/kids/quake.htm>

Global Earthquake Response Center.
<http://www.earthquakes.com>

USGS Earthquakes for Kids.
<http://earthquakes.usgs.gov/4kids/>

Index

A

aftershocks, 16
Alpine belt, 15

B

borehole tiltmeter, 12

C

Chena, 29, 30
continental plates.
      See tectonic
      plates.

E

earthquake kit, 36
earthquakes
      Alaska, 18–19,
            29–32, 33
      animal prediction
            of, 5, 6, 35
      Bolivia, 17
      California, 32–33
      Chile, 18, 30
      China, 22
      El Salvador, 19
      intensity of, 13
      Iran, 25–26
      Japan, 24–25
      magnitude of,
            13–14, 34
      Peru, 19, 21
      prediction of, 9,
            16, 34–35
      regions of activity,
            14–16
      Sumatra,
            Indonesia, 26

surviving, 35–38
      Turkey, 5–9, 38
epicenter, 12, 30

F

fault line, 11
fault zones, 34
focus, 11, 12
foreshocks, 16, 34,
      35

G

Good Friday Quake,
      The, 29–32

H

Heng, Zhang, 12

I

Indian Ocean, 26, 28

L

landslides, 17, 19,
      21, 30

M

moment magnitude
      scale (M), 13–14

N

North Anatolian
      Fault, 8

O

oceanic plates. *See*
      tectonic plates.

P

Pacific belt, 14–15
Pacific Rim, 23, 34
plate boundaries, 11,

16, 33
plate tectonics,
      10–11
point of origin. *See*
      focus.

R

Richter magnitude
      scale, 13
Ring of Fire. *See*
      Pacific Rim.

S

San Andreas Fault,
      32
satellites, 12, 14
search and rescue
      dogs, 41
search and rescue
      workers, 38–41
seismic trucks, 12
seismic waves,
      11–12, 13
seismographs, 12,
      14
seismologists, 12, 35
seismology, 12–14
seismometer, 12–13
slide zone, 19

T

tectonic plates,
      10–11, 14, 17,
      24–25
tremors, 8, 10, 30
tsunamis, 18–19,
      26, 28, 30